WOMEN WHO CHANGED
THEIR WORLD

WOMEN WHO CHANGED THEIR WORLD

VICTOR BOOKS ®

A DIVISION OF SCRIPTURE PRESS PUBLICATIONS INC.
USA CANADA ENGLAND

Recommended Dewey Decimal Classification: 248.833
Suggested Subject Heading: PERSONAL CHRISTIANITY FOR WOMEN

Library of Congress Catalog Card Number: 90-20534
ISBN: 0-89693-001-7

 3   4   5   6   7   8   9   10 Printing/Year   95   94   93   92

VICTOR BOOKS
A division of SP Publications, Inc.
          Wheaton, Illinois 60187

•CONTENTS•

*Recognition to Beth Donigan Seversen
for assistance
in researching and formulating
parts of this book.*

•INTRODUCTION•

Women's needs are the same throughout the ages. They need to belong, to love and be loved, find their identity, develop their gifts, maintain a good attitude, juggle responsibilities, and learn to forgive and accept forgiveness.

The women in this study do a little bit of all these things. We can learn from their triumphs and failures. Women can change their world—for the better or for the worse. With Christ, we can make a good difference.

•BEFORE YOU BEGIN•

People who gather together for Bible study are likely to be at different places in their spiritual lives, and their study materials should be flexible enough to meet their different needs. This book is designed to be used as a Bible study guide for such groups in homes or churches. It can also be used by individuals who are studying on their own. The lessons are written in five distinct sections, so that they can be used in a variety of situations. Groups and individuals alike can choose to use the elements they find most useful in the order they find most beneficial.

These studies will help you learn some new truths from the Bible as well as how to dig out those truths. You will learn not only *what* the Bible says, but how to use Scripture to deepen your relationship with Jesus Christ by obeying it and applying it in daily living. These studies will also provide an opportunity for potential leaders to learn how to lead a discussion in a nonthreatening setting.

What You'll Need
For each study you will need a Bible and this Bible study guide. You might also want to have a notebook in which to record your thoughts and discoveries from your personal study and group meetings. A notebook could also be used to record prayer requests from the group.

The Sections
Food for Thought. This is a devotional narrative that introduces the topic, person, or passage featured in the lesson. There are several ways it can be used. Each person could read it before coming to the group meeting, and someone could briefly summarize it at the beginning. It could be read silently by each person at the beginning of the session, or it could be read aloud, by one or several group members. (Suggested time: 10 minutes)

Talking It Over. This section contains discussion questions to help you review what you learned in Food for Thought. There are also questions to help you apply the narrative's truths to daily life. The person who leads the discussion of these questions need not be a trained or experienced teacher. All that is needed is someone to keep things moving and facilitate group interaction. (Suggested time: 30 minutes)

Praying It Through. This is a list of suggestions for prayer based on the lesson. You may want to use all the suggestions or eliminate some in order to leave more time for personal sharing and prayer requests. (Suggested time: 20 minutes)

Digging Deeper. The questions in this section are also related to the passage, topic, or character from the lesson. But they will not always be limited to the exact passage or character from Food for Thought. Passages and characters from both the Old and New Testaments will appear in this section, in order to show how God has worked through *all* of history in people's lives. These questions will require a little more thinking and some digging into Scripture, as well as some use of Bible study tools. Participants will be stretched as they become experienced in the "how-tos" of Bible study. (Suggested time: 45 minutes)

Tool Chest. The Tool Chest contains a description of a specific type of Bible study help and includes an explanation of how it is used. An example of the tool is given, and an example of it or excerpt from it is usually included in the Digging Deeper study.

The Bible study helps in the Tool Chest can be purchased by anyone who desires to build a basic library of Bible study reference books and other tools. They would also be good additions to a church library. Some are reasonably inexpensive, but others are quite expensive. A few may be available in your local library or in a seminary or college library. A group might decide to purchase one tool during each series and build a corporate tool chest for all the members of the group to use. You can never be too young a Christian to begin to master Bible study helps, nor can you be too old to learn new methods of rightly dividing the Word of truth.

Options for Group Use

Different groups, made up of people at diverse stages of spiritual growth, will want to use the elements in this book in different ways. Here are a few suggestions to get you started, but be creative and sensitive to your group's needs.

☐ Spend 5-15 minutes at the beginning of the group time introducing yourselves and having group members answer an icebreaker question. (Sample icebreaker questions are included under Tips for Leaders.)

☐ Extend the prayer time to include sharing of prayer requests, praise items, or things group members have learned recently in their times of personal Bible study.

☐ The leader could choose questions for discussion from the Digging Deeper section based on whether participants have prepared ahead of time or not.

☐ The entire group could break into smaller groups to allow different groups to use different sections. (The smaller groups could move to other rooms in the home or church where you are meeting.)

Tips for Leaders

Preparation

1. Pray for the Holy Spirit's guidance as you study, that you will be equipped to teach the lesson and make it appealing and applicable.

2. Read through the entire lesson and any Bible passages orverses that are mentioned. Answer all the questions.

3. Become familiar enough with the lesson that, if time in the group is running out, you know which questions could most easily be left out.

4. Gather all the items you will need for the study: name tags, extra pens, extra Bibles.

The Meeting

1. Start and end on time.

2. Have everyone wear a name tag until group members know one another's names.

3. Have each person introduce himself or herself, or ask regular attenders to introduce guests.

4. For each meeting, pick an icebreaker question or another activity to help group members get to know one another better.

5. Use any good ideas to make everyone feel comfortable.

The Discussion

1. Ask the questions, but try to let the group answer. Don't be afraid of silence. Reword the question if it is unclear to the group or answer it yourself to clarify.

2. Encourage everyone to participate. If someone is shy, ask that person to answer a nonthreatening question or give an opinion. If someone tends to monopolize the discussion, thank that person for his or her contribution and ask if someone else has anything he or she would like to add. (Or ask that person to make the coffee!)

3. If someone gives an incorrect answer, don't bluntly or tactlessly tell him or her so. If it is partly right, reinforce that. Ask if anyone else has any thoughts on the subject. (Disagree agreeably!)

4. Avoid tangents. If someone is getting off the subject, ask that person how his or her point relates to the lesson.

5. Don't feel threatened if someone asks a question you can't answer. Tell the person you don't know but will find out before the next meeting—then be sure to find out! Or ask if someone would like to research and present the answer at the group's next meeting.

Icebreaker Questions

The purpose of these icebreaker questions is to help the people in your group get to know one another over the course of the study. The questions you use when your group members don't know one another very well should be very general and nonthreatening. As time goes on, your questions can become more focused and specific. Always give group members the option of passing if they think a question is too personal.

What do you like to do for fun?
What is your favorite season? dessert? book?
What would be your ideal vacation?
What exciting thing happened to you this week?
What was the most memorable thing you did with your family when you were a child?

What one word best describes the way you feel today?

Tell three things you are thankful for.

Imagine that your house is on fire. What three things would you try to take with you on your way out?

If you were granted one wish, what would it be?

What experience of your past would you most enjoy reliving?

What quality do you most appreciate in a friend?

What is your pet peeve?

What is something you are learning to do or trying to get better at?

What is your greatest hope?

What is your greatest fear?

What one thing would you like to change about yourself?

What has been the greatest accomplishment of your life?

What has been the greatest disappointment of your life?

Need More Help?

Here is a list of books that contain helpful information on leading discussions and working in groups:

> *How to Lead Small Group Bible Studies* (NavPress, 1982).
> *Creative Bible Learning for Adults,* Monroe Marlowe and Bobbie Reed (Regal, 1977).
> *Getting Together,* Em Griffin (InterVarsity Press, 1982).
> *Good Things Come in Small Groups* (InterVarsity Press, 1985).

One Last Thought

This book is a tool you can use whether you have one or one hundred people who want to study the Bible and whether you have one or no teachers. Don't wait for a brilliant Bible study leader to appear—most such teachers acquired their skills by starting with a book like this and learning as they went along. Torrey said, "The best way to begin, is to begin." Happy beginnings!

1
Changing Her World Through Sin
(Eve)

•FOOD FOR THOUGHT•

The Bible is the story of man's (male and female) identity. That identity is revealed in creation, obscured in the Fall, and renewed through redemption. If we are searching for a reason for being, we will find our answers in the Word of God.

Eve was having an identity crisis. "So what's new?" you may ask. "My teenage daughter has one of those every morning before breakfast." Well, the reason your teenage daughter is troubled with her identity is simple. We females are all daughters of Eve!

What *is* an identity anyway? The dictionary defines it as "the condition of being the same as something or someone," or "to make identification of oneself to someone else." The women of the 90s are looking to the media, marriage, or modern philosophies for that identification.

They are fascinated with Lady Di, Madonna, Roseanne, and the lifestyles of the rich and famous. They look for models to "match" their dreams and fantasies in the worlds of the soaps or novels. The idea of two becoming "one flesh" appeals to many because of the idea of totally identifying with another person. But when marriage fades and our identity has been only in that marriage—we are in deep trouble. Likewise, if our identity has been in our children, we flounder when they leave home!

In the 50s Betty Friedan wrote, "The problem for women today is not sexual, but a problem of identity." She advised women to find the answer in themselves. So women tried—and failed—for God never intended that to be possible! Shirley MacLaine and a plethora of New Age gurus tell us we must identify with the "cosmos," with Mother

Earth, or seek a mystical oneness with spirit life, yet Mother Earth is not the answer to our search for Someone "bigger" than ourselves, for we are undoubtedly "bigger" than Mother Earth. The believer in Christ says loud and clear to the woman of the 90s, "You only find your true identity when you have a relationship with the God who gave you an identity like His!" (Gen. 1:26-27) Eve knew her reason for being was to identify closely with the God who had designed her for that purpose, and in Genesis 1 we see her happily enjoying that relationship.

Eve was created perfect woman. She had a perfect understanding of who she was and why she was what she was. In Genesis 2, she was given a job to do and never felt she had to shop around to find a better one, because she believed an intelligent God had created her with an intelligent reason in mind. She felt significant and important, and she loved her work. Worship was work and work was worship. It was paradise to wake up on Monday mornings!

Many women of the 90s are dissatisfied with their jobs. If a woman's identity is in her work alone, wait till she's fired! When her identity is in God, however, she will rest in the fact that He designed her for a specific work task, and finding and submitting to that will release her to be all she's meant to be, whether it be at home, in the work force, or both.

Eve's work was to receive God's blessings through unbroken fellowship with Him, replenish the earth through the bearing of children, and rule over God's creation with Adam in harmony, partnership, and equality.

She was to be his "helper" (the Hebrew word *ecer* being used in Deuteronomy 33:7, 26, and 29 and in many other places as the word for God, the "Helper" of Israel). She was a suitable match, an ideal partner. Some see a hierarchy in Genesis 1–2 and cite the fact that Adam named the woman and she was created second. But *naming* does not necessarily suppose authority in this case as the word *woman* is a descriptive word describing her origins.

Adam himself was created second to the animals but that does not mean he was inferior to them! Someone has said Eve was not taken from Adam's head to rule over him, or from his feet to be trampled, but from his side to be an equal partner. Genesis 1 gives us a powerful statement of the equality of the sexes as God intended it to be, and Genesis 2 gives a description of it working as God intended it to work. If there is headship before the Fall, I believe it is there to ensure that equality and partnership are practiced.

So God made the man and woman to compliment each other—as

companions and not competitors. In Genesis 2, Adam and Eve are doing everything right in an "all right world"—but then comes Genesis 3 and Eve's identity crisis. Eve's identity revealed in creation is now obscured in the Fall. The image is broken.

What *is* an image? An image has a resemblance to an archetype. It reflects or mirrors like a shadow, or stamps the likeness of the archetype on a coin. Christ, the Bible tells us in Colossians 1:15 and 2 Corinthians 4:4, is "the image of the invisible God" to created beings.

Now we are not like God in the way that Christ is like God, but we bear His image in the sense that we are personal, rational, and moral beings as He is. We are like the Trinity in its plurality in that the man that God created comes as male and female—plurality. In this way we *both* reflect His image. This image, moreover, is not found in the animals. They reflect His genius but not His image. It is personality that makes us unique—a rationality and responsibility to moral law that sets us apart. Eve knew God was her Image Maker. She knew too that she was the image breaker!

Eve, the world's first iconoclast, or identity wrecker, was deceived by the serpent into believing she could become an independent image. The shadow didn't need the substance, the snake assured her! Her mistake lay in believing she could be good, enjoy pleasure, and be wise, all independently of God who is the sum totality of all these things. We don't know if Eve had received all the information that Adam had been given concerning the tree of the knowledge of good and evil, but the snake obviously determined that she was his best bet. He deceived her into thinking she could be like God in the sense of being totally independent like He was! Why was she deceived? Because she was dumber than Adam? Inferior to Adam? Less spiritual than her counterpart? Rather, I believe, because she was out of her league. Gil Bilezikian in his book, *Beyond Sex Roles* (Baker), says, "Eve did not sin willfully, but was fooled into making a fateful error of judgment. God held Adam responsible—he was not 'deceived' by the woman, but willfully caused the race to fall" (Rom. 5:12-14; 1 Cor. 15:22).

This is important, for as John Stott says, "As a result of the fall, headship has degenerated into domination and subjugation, and mistreatment of woman throughout the ages." In some countries women are "covered." They are considered "deceivers" of men. They are blamed for generating lust and men's downfall. They have been regarded as deceivers, not the deceived.

And so God said to the woman, "I will greatly increase your pains in childbearing; with pain you will give birth to children. Your desire will be for your husband, and he will rule over you" (Gen. 3:16).

Is this a descriptive passage, or a prescriptive passage? Is God saying this is His *prescription* for how to put things right, or is it His *description* of how things will be between the sexes as a result of sin? Herein lies part of the debate that splits the evangelical world! Arguments can convincingly be made theologically for *both* the hierarchical and egalitarian point of view drawn from this passage alone, and much study will only go to show the whole subject is certainly not as clear as it seems to some.

It is enough to say here that the woman was not cursed and neither was Adam. The snake was cursed and Christ was promised to become our Curse on the cross (Gen. 3:15) that the curse of death may be destroyed. In the Cross and the community of the redeemed, one of God's intentions is to restore His original design of mutuality in equality between the sexes. Rolling back the results of the Fall becomes the church's challenge.

So one of the results of the Fall—suffering—in practical Christian living is to be overcome by research, medicine, and healing ministries. The land that was affected is to be cultivated and worked to produce food for starving nations, and male headship is to become such a source of help, love, and sacrificial giving that female partnership may be nourished, flourishing under such encouragement and direction as God originally intended (Eph. 5).

We women are all daughters of Eve. Let us not forget it! We must never take on the snake on our own. We, like Eve, are no match for his subtlety and his devices haven't changed. We are women with an identity made in God's image and after His likeness, and though our first mother and father fell and broke that image, it has been restored in Christ who is God's remedy for sin and its results. Our family, church, and community relationships should feel the impact of that salvation. In the beginning an earthly paradise was lost, but at the end a heavenly paradise awaits those who will accept God's Christ as their Saviour.

•TALKING IT OVER•

---

1. REVIEW EVE'S IDENTITY.
   □ Define identity. Cite ways women of the 90s look for their identities.
   □ Read Genesis 1:26-31. Discuss Eve's paradise. What was so perfect about it?

10 minutes

---

2. REVIEW EVE'S INDUSTRY.
   Read Genesis 2:18-25.
   □ What can we learn about work, as God intended it to be, from this passage?
   □ What can we learn about Adam and Eve's ideal relationship?

10 minutes

---

3. REVIEW EVE'S IMAGE.
   Read Genesis 3:1-13.
   □ In verse 6, what was so bad about her action? What were the results of her Fall?
   Discuss Genesis 3:15-16 in relation to the Cross.
   □ What was God's covenant promise?
   □ What does Christ desire as far as men and women relationships are concerned now?

10 minutes

•PRAYING IT THROUGH•

Suggested Times

---

1. (As a group) Praise God for all the things He planned for men and women in creation.

4 minutes

---

2. (On your own) Pray for women's full identity to be restored in reality as women find Christ.

4 minutes

---

3. (In pairs) Pray for women under domination of men in:
   □ governments
   □ marriages
   □ work situations

4 minutes

---

4. (As a group) Pray for men to see women as God sees them.

4 minutes

---

5. (On your own) Pray for Christian women to model new relationships in their lives.

4 minutes

• DIGGING DEEPER •

Jezebel

One characteristic of fine literature is honesty. Characters who are either completely good or completely bad do not generally portray reality. The Scriptures exude integrity by presenting to the reader real women who struggled between good and evil and who did not always make right choices. Eve and Jezebel are two examples of women who adversely influenced their worlds. As you compare their lives, let them be your mentors. What can you learn from their errors?

Jezebel was a woman who had a vast influence on her world as Queen of northern Israel. Her life was a sad and grim commentary on the consequences of using power and prestige for evil ends.

1. Consult a Bible help (Bible dictionary, Study Bible, or Commentary) for the meaning behind the name *Jezebel.*
   perhaps - unexalted, unhusbanded

   Read the following references to Jezebel and build a character sketch of her using only nouns in your description: 1 Kings 16:31; 18:4-19; 19:1-2; 21:5-25; 2 Kings 9. worshiper of Baal, killer, deciever, trouble maker

   How do her disposition, motivation, and intentions belie her name? She is evil

2. Look up the following terms in a Bible dictionary. Explain how they impact your understanding of the historical setting during Jezebel's reign.

   Ethbaal — King of Sidon; Father of Jezebel

   Phoenicians — Worshiped many gods.

   Baal — used to be a common term for husband, sometimes when people worshiped Baal they sacraficed their children, the priests used to dance around the alters and cut themselves with knives

19

Ashtaroth/Astorte - *refers to many local goddess*

Ahab - *Son of Omri + the 7th king of nothern Isreal, 22 years*

3. What devastating sin did Ahab commit and how did it affect the course of history? (cf. Judges 2:11; 1 Kings 11:2; 16:31-33)

Served Baal, + married Jezebel

Is there a warning or command in Scripture you are not heeding?

4. Jezebel identified with whose image? What was her passion and how did she supply it?

Satan, murder

5. How did she misuse her gifts and strengths?

Used them for evil

6. List the consequences of her actions exhibited in her family and in the nation of Israel.

Ahab

died on vinyard

Athaliah (2 Kings 8:26; 11; 2 Chronicles 22; 23:13-21; 24:7)

Was slain

Ahaziah (1 Kings 22:51-53; 2 Kings 1:1-18)

He followed his parents and ended up dying

Jehoram (2 Kings 9:14-24)

Was killed by Jehu

Northern Kingdom (Micah 6:16)
destroyed because they followed her actions

7. What lessons does the story of Naboth's vineyard teach us? (1 Kings 21) *Do not follow someone elses evil lead but follow God.*

   Do not be greedy

8. How are you like Jezebel? Is your passion misdirected? What can you learn from Jezebel's life?

   power corupts

9. Give examples of how your actions have affected those you influence for good and evil.

10. Ask God to help you influence your family in a positive way (cf. 2 Timothy 1:5; 1 Peter 1:13-16; 3:1-2).

For Further Study
1. Choose another woman in Scripture who adversely influenced her world and do a character study on her life. What lessons can you learn and evils can you avoid from her negative example?
2. What is Jezebel a proverb for in modern times?

•TOOL CHEST•
(A Suggested Optional Resource)

DAUGHTERS OF THE CHURCH

Daughters of the Church by Ruth A. Tucker and Walter L. Liefeld is a systematic chronological study of women and their ministries from the days of Christ Jesus to modern times. You will be introduced in this text to numerous women who have changed their world throughout church history, beginning with Mary, the mother of Jesus, and concluding with influential women who served Christ during the decade of the 1980s. Topics such as women in missions, women in the non-Western church, and the women's issue facing the contemporary church are explored. This book is beautifully illustrated and is available in paperback.

2
Changing Her World Through Meekness
(Sarah)

•FOOD FOR THOUGHT•

Sarah was a royal lady, and yet a royal rebel! It took God 127 years to finish His beautiful work in Sarah's life! Change takes time. As I read Sarah's story, I am struck by one thing above all others—God cannot change an uncooperative person! It takes Him time and trouble to make a royal out of a rebel, but God, who has all the time in the world, can afford to wait. He will not impose His will on ours.

Sarah is given to us as an example of such cooperation. First Peter 3:6 tells us she had a meek and quiet spirit. And yet, as we read the account of Sarah's life, she seems to be neither meek nor quiet. We are told she called Abraham "Lord," or "Adonai," which means *master*, and we are urged to be "her daughters" and follow in her steps. But how does this exactly relate to the woman of the 90s who may or may not be married to an Abraham?

The word *meek* does not mean "weak," but rather the opposite. The idea is a wild horse tamed—controlled by a loving master. The word *quiet* carries the idea of a willingness to be instructed and to learn. Jesus was described as "meek" in spirit. He was in no way weak! He had about His person a sense of harnessed strength and power.

Sarai's given name gives us a clue as to her nature. Her name is derived from the same root as the word *Israel* and can mean "striving or contentiousness." It carries the notion of strife and dispute.

Undoubtedly Sarah's story confirms these ideas about her character. In Genesis 16:1-6, we find her disputing with Hagar (her maidservant), arguing with Abraham (her husband), while a few chapters before in Genesis 18:10-15, she quarrels with the Almighty Himself! She appears to be a lively, feisty woman, with a turbulent spirit!

She was lively and she was lovely. Her husband, finding himself in hostile territory and fearing for his life, asked her to tell a half-truth for him. "I know thou art fair to look upon," he said. He asked her to say she was his sister, which was partly true in that she was his half-sister! This way Abraham hoped the men of these foreign cultures would not kill him in order to possess her. This actually happened twice, first with King Abimelech and later with Pharaoh of Egypt. And all of this when Sarah was well over 80 years of age! I suppose such beauty as Sarah's is not to be envied when it causes such trauma! However, Peter tells us Sarah was beautiful inwardly as well as outwardly. That God looked on her heart. Her beauty lay not in the merely physical, but in her spirit or attitude as well. If this is true, and we must believe it as Scripture says so, how and when did God change such a lively, lovely liar into a woman with a meek and quiet nature? God changed her name to Sarah—Princess—as surely as He changed her character which had caused such strife (Gen. 17:15-16).

Sarah's mistake in lying for Abraham was that she was loyal to a fault. She was so committed to Abraham, she was not able to see this did not mean being committed to doing the wrong thing. But God saw her commitment to her man, his mission, and her marriage, and used these very things over the long term to refine her character. Deep down Sarah really wanted to be God's woman. She wanted to cooperate with God. Now that's exactly the sort of person God can work with.

God certainly does not want us to tell lies for our husbands like Sarah did. This is not what a submissive attitude is all about! We are not called to submit to wrong doing. We need to remind ourselves that man—male and female—created in the image of God fell, and headship, responsible to keep the sexes in harmony and compatible with each other in partnership and equality, degenerated into domination. If your husband tries to dominate you and tell you to do something that contradicts God's Law, as Abraham asked Sarah to do, then you need to "obey God rather than men" (Acts 5:29) and say no—meekly, of course!

Peter himself balances his statements about Sarah by saying we are "heirs together of the gracious gift of eternal life." Part of our inheritance together is to encourage each other to do the *right* thing, not the *wrong* thing. So what does the Bible mean when it calls us to be daughters of Sarah? I believe it calls us to emulate her basic attitude of cooperation with God, allowing Him a chance to change us.

We need to realize though that submission means different things in different situations. Michael Griffiths says the same word cannot mean the same thing in five different categories. For example, he points out that the Bible says we should submit to the state (Rom. 13:1), wives to husbands (Eph. 5:22), children to parents (Eph. 6; Luke 2:51), and slaves to masters (Eph. 6:5). Obviously a woman is not to submit to her own husband as a slave does to his master! A child will not submit to his father as he will to the President. New relationships under the New Covenant enable a husband to be responsible to Christ as his head, to roll back the results of the Fall, and to listen with respect to his wife's opinion as an equal partner in the kingdom's work. New relationships lived out between Christians mean it's all joy to esteem others better than ourselves and be servants for Jesus' sake, whatever our age, marital status, or gender. If only Sarah had been able to encourage Abraham in his moments of weakness and refuse to lie for him, they would both have been spared the embarrassment of Pharaoh's and Abimelech's public rebuke, and God's name would not have been dishonored. So submission means different things to different people at different times. It never means we submit to any old thing. For the single woman, it means something other than for the married woman, but for all of us, men and women alike, an initial submission to God as our Saviour and Lord must come first. Then He will help us to bend our strong will to His desire. Sarah learned to listen and to obey. She was teachable, and the Lord loved her for that. How do we develop this attitude? Are we teachable or argumentative and stubborn?

First, we need to dress our souls in daily prayer. We must strip down spiritually each day and then decide that we are going to dress our souls as thoroughly and carefully as we physically dress our bodies.

Second, we must decide to be teachable. Sarah laughed at God when He told her something that was hard to believe (Gen. 18:12). She learned over time to trust God's word, to quit arguing, and simply accept His promises by faith. We choose to be either a handful or a handmaid!! If we give God control of the wild donkey inside us and decide to respond rather than react to the people around us, the One who changed Sarah will change us and transform us into His image!

Third, we can also welcome situations that cause us to depend on God. Sarah had a lifetime of learning to submit to circumstances beyond her control and that she could not change. Because of her meek and quiet spirit those very situations were used in the hand of God to fashion her after His own heart.

Finally, we can rejoice when we have an opportunity to serve—anyone! Husband, parents, children, grandchildren, neighbors, friends, fellow believers, even enemies. *Service* is another word for submission.

Jesus Himself came not to be served but to serve (Mark 10:45). We serve people by doing the right thing for them—by listening, relieving, caring, helping, and sometimes by even saying no. In a gentle and meek way! I know no quicker way of growing a royal princess inside a contentious woman than this!

•TALKING IT OVER•

1. READ AND DISCUSS 1 PETER 3:1-7.
   Freely discuss Peter's comments concerning:
   ☐ Wives with unbelieving husbands
   ☐ Sarah's example

   10 minutes

2. WORK IN GROUPS OR PAIRS.
   Read Genesis 16:1-6 and 18:10-15.
   ☐ Imagine you are God. What do you feel about Sarah?
   ☐ Imagine you are Sarah. Do you have sympathy with her reactions? Why?
   ☐ Imagine you are Hagar. How are you feeling?
   ☐ Imagine you are Abraham. How about you?
   Pool your findings with the whole group. Summarize conclusions.

   10 minutes

3. DISCUSS.
   How do we practically:
   ☐ Dress our soul in daily prayer?
   ☐ Decide to be teachable?
   ☐ Welcome situations that cause us to depend on God?
   ☐ Give God the *reign* of our spirit?

   10 minutes

•PRAYING IT THROUGH•

Suggested Times

1. (On your own) Quietly meditate on 1 Peter 3:1-6. Thank God for the parts of the study that helped you.

5 minutes

2. (As a group) Pray for others facing situations they cannot change:
   ☐ In their marriage
   ☐ With childlessness
   ☐ With uncontrolled temperaments and bad attitudes

10 minutes

3. (In twos) Share a pertinent prayer need. Pray for each other. Finish with prayers concerning a "meek and quiet spirit" for yourselves.

5 minutes

•DIGGING DEEPER•

Priscilla

By now you will have noticed that each **Digging Deeper** section explores a woman different (yet alike in many ways) from the one discussed in the **Food for Thought** section. The Scriptures are brimming over with women who teach us by example, and each has a relevant lesson for us today. You have an opportunity to get to know not just eight women, but 16 women in the Bible who will acquaint you with spiritual truths by their role models. Enjoy spending an hour or so with each and glean all she has to say. Compare and contrast the two women paired in each chapter. Consider other female examples in Scripture that come to mind as you study. Imagine what instructions, warnings, and exhortations these women would share if they were seated at your coffee table.

1. Recall a teacher who was extremely influential in your life. What about him/her impressed you?

2. While Sarah exhibited a "teachable" spirit, the Spirit actually used Priscilla to teach the Scriptures alongside her husband, Aquila. Why would a teacher need to be teachable himself? Read Priscilla's story in Acts 18:2-4, 24-26; Romans 16:3-5; 1 Corinthians 16:19; and 2 Timothy 4:19.

   If he wasn't teachable than he would already know every thing.

3. We learned in the "Food for Thought" section that Sarah was committed to "her man, his mission, and her marriage." How was Priscilla a "daughter" of Sarah in each of these categories? Give references to support your answer.

   They started a church together

   2 Tim 4:19
   1 Cor. 16:19

   What do you admire about her marriage?

   How they loved eachother and always were a team

4. What services did Priscilla and her husband render to the church?

Acts 18:2-4

tents

Acts 18:18-19

traveled with Paul

Acts 18:24-26

told Apollos the rest of the message

Romans 16:3-5

risked their lives

1 Corinthians 16:19

Church meets in their house

5. Identify Priscilla's spiritual gifts and note how she used them for the glory of God. *love, patience, kindness, faithfulness*

6. How did she employ the practical skills and abilities she had mastered? *to be an example to others*

7. Priscilla and her husband were "run out of Rome." They lived in Corinth for a time and then accompanied Paul by ship to Syria and ministered in Ephesus. Chart their travels on a map. What qualities would Priscilla most likely have developed to be involved in such a transient ministry? Put yourself in her situation and mention a few things that would be difficult for you personally. *sacrifice*

8. Prominence is often given to Priscilla's leadership because her name appears many times before her husband's. Consult a Bible help and give two or three variant reasons for her name being found first. Which answer is most supported by the text?

9. As a couple, Aquila and Priscilla had an effective teaching and discipling ministry. Give an example of how they multiplied their ministry (Acts 18:24-28; 1 Cor. 1:12).

    they told Apollos the rest of the message and he spreaded it

10. In what areas would you prefer to be more like Priscilla? How might you improve your stewardship of the abilities God has entrusted to you? Are you multiplying the spiritual gifts God has given you? What legacy would you like to leave behind?

For Further Study
1. Take a spiritual gifts inventory and ask your pastor or wise Christian friend to help you assess your gifts.
2. Make an effort to use your home this month to benefit the body of Christ.

•TOOL CHEST•
(A Suggested Optional Resource)

JONI EARECKSON TADA
Despite her handicap, Joni Eareckson Tada is changing her world. In 1967 Joni suffered a diving accident which left her a quadriplegic. Through her personal struggles, she has developed an intimate and committed relationship with God. Today Joni is making an impact on her world for Christ through films, books, speaking, and painting. Not only an evangelist, Joni lives what she preaches. She is actively working to raise our nation's conscious awareness of the disabled and their needs through her ministry, Joni and Friends. Her books include *Joni, A Step Further, Choices . . . Changes,* and *Glorious Intruder.*

3
Changing Her World Through Her Gifts
(Miriam)

•FOOD FOR THOUGHT•

Miriam was courageous. She needed to be. She lived in Egypt in dark and terrible days. The throne was now ruled by a Pharaoh who did not know her ancestor Joseph, who had used his position in Egypt to keep his people safe. Now everyone slaved for the new king. Cruelty was the order of the day. Whips were used on Jewish backs and cries went up to heaven for help. Along with her people, Miriam learned to pray! God heard their cries for help (Ex. 2:24) and had pity on them.

Pharaoh had ordered all Hebrew baby boys be thrown into the River Nile. Miriam helped her parents, Amram and Jochebed, to hide their beautiful new baby till he was too big to hide. Then they put the babe in an ark on the Nile, where Pharaoh's daughter made it her habit to bathe. Miriam waited on the bank and watched to see what would happen to her brother. How she must have wept when she heard her baby brother crying. And she must have wondered too about the crocodiles! Pharaoh's daughter drew Moses out of the water, and Miriam showed great initiative in suggesting a Hebrew nurse be found for the babe. Pharaoh's daughter who was sorry for the little baby agreed, and Miriam ran quickly and fetched her own mother!

God had designed Miriam with a specific task in mind, equipping her to do it. She was a courageous and quick-thinking child, with a rich, spiritual family heritage. Miriam's father, Amram, was descended from Abraham and is mentioned along with his wife in Hebrews as part of God's gallery of heroes. In this exciting chapter, the Bible tells us that Amram and Jochebed were not afraid of the king's commandment and were full of faith (Heb. 11:23).

We need to follow their example no matter how difficult or dangerous things get for our children, and be full of faith and fortitude. Then, hopefully, we shall see our own children grow up to love and serve the Lord too. Miriam saw God answer her parents' prayers and her own in an extraordinary way.

Miriam learned four basic lessons in Egypt. First, she learned that God's word could be relied upon. Apparently the Lord had promised her parents deliverance and they understood Moses would have a part in that. Second, she learned that God answers prayer. Third, she learned that God uses human instruments to do His will and that He never calls without equipping. He doesn't mind if His people are tall or short, thin or fat, black or white, old or young. All He asks is a willing heart, a ready mind, and committed hands. He will do the rest! Fourth, she learned all these things in troubled times. Her God proved to be a very present and adequate help in the darkest of days. Miriam had lots of time to test the faithfulness of God. It would be 40 years before Moses grew up and fled from Pharaoh's palace, and another 40 until he returned to Egypt to lead his people to freedom. During this time Amram and Jochebed died while Aaron and Miriam slaved alongside the Israelites.

The next time we meet Miriam in the Scriptures, Moses has returned to lead his people into Canaan and they have just passed safely through the Red Sea. She is one of God's appointed leaders of the Exodus. It is estimated 600,000 people went to Egypt. Moses was their prophet and lawgiver, Aaron their high priest, and Miriam their prophetess! These three provided spiritual leadership and guidance for everyone. The Bible tells us that God Himself classed Miriam as one of the three great leaders of Israel (Micah 6:4). Women were not excluded from the prophetic office in the Old Testament. Hannah, Huldah, and Isaiah's wife are other examples.

A Hebrew prophet proclaimed God's word, made prophetic revelations about the present or the future, preached, encouraged, comforted, and counseled. There is a current debate on this issue. Do women have these same gifts under the New Covenant? If so, how does a modern Miriam use her gifts in the church? The debate ranges around a few texts, 1 Timothy 2:11-15 being one of them. It says, "A woman should learn in quietness and full submission. I do not permit a woman to teach or to have authority over a man; she must be silent. For Adam was formed first, then Eve. And Adam was not the one deceived; it was the woman who was deceived and became a sinner."

Our denomination or Christian cultural background will probably be a big factor in determining how we view this particular verse. Suffice it to say, the surface meaning of it seems to contradict other Pauline material and indicates this situation was an "occasional" occasion and one which led to an occasional epistle from the apostle.

Dake's Bible summarizes what was happening in the Ephesian church, which is the backdrop to Paul's letter to Timothy. Women were being proud, bossy, and lording it over everyone else. Dake says in his footnote, "Women should not dictate to men, but exercise their rights to teach, prophesy, or preach, pray, and do other things, under the authority of men."

Miriam was not a married woman. (Incidentally, some think that 1 Timothy 2 was addressed to married women and not to single women or not to all women.) Moses, however, was the man God had put in authority over Israel, including Aaron and Miriam. Together Moses, Aaron, and Miriam led Israel. God had certainly spoken as clearly through Aaron and Miriam as He had through Moses. I don't see how this can be disputed.

But one day Miriam overstepped her boundaries and usurped Moses' authority. Yes, she was a leader and a teacher—of men as well as women—but she had been given someone to be accountable to—her younger brother in this case. One day she used the occasion of her brother's marriage to a Cushite woman as an opportunity to lord it over Moses and covet his position. She also took Aaron right along with her (Num. 12:1-2).

I must confess I have often wondered why it was only Miriam who was struck with leprosy at this point and not Aaron, as they both took part in this rebellion. I have come to realize that this was not because she was a woman, but because she was the instigator, and her younger brother simply went along with her. Pride so often begins, as in this case, with a critical spirit, develops into a covetous spirit and becomes extremely dangerous. We have to remember Moses was Miriam's "baby" brother and so was Aaron, so it must have been hard for her to forget that—but pride has no place in the Lord's business and especially among His leaders, whether they be men or women. It had to be dealt with severely so that Israel would learn humility.

The privileged authority that God gives to a Miriam must be treated with extreme meekness and exercised in the fear of the Lord. Moses was exercising this authority just like that as Numbers 12 is careful to tell us. Miriam, however, had allowed pride to bring about a fall. She and her brother had grumbled about Moses. Why should he get all the recognition for his spiritual gifts, they asked each other. Aren't *our* gifts just as important and impressive?

God's gifts are God's gifts, so why should we ever get personally proud about them? It could be that God's gifting of 70 elders with prophetic powers had been a threatening thing to Miriam and Aaron too (Num. 11:17). Anyway, God summoned Moses, Aaron, and Miriam to a meeting with Him, and Miriam was seen to be white with leprosy after their rendezvous.

Pride is like leprosy and necessitates a cooling-off period! Miriam, therefore, was sent outside the camp for seven days. After this, forgiven and restored, God answered Moses' prayer on her behalf and healed her. Israel did not travel on until she was brought back among them. Sometimes, as possibly in the Ephesian church, God has to put proud people in their place. He removes them from their positions and withdraws His power. But He also forgives and restores His gifted people. It's hard to preach and teach when you're proud. It can be done, of course, but nothing of eternal significance will be accomplished! Little fruit will remain.

Twice in the biblical account of Miriam's life the Bible says, "God heard." He heard the peoples cry for deliverance and He heard the proud, rebellious talk against His appointed leader, Moses. He answered both these cries. Today He delivers His people from punishment, but He also delivers His people from pride. Our God is a hearing, helping, healing, yet *holy* God. After Miriam's lapse, she returned to lead Israel alongside her two brothers for 38 more years. They were weary years, and she was not to enter Canaan, but I believe they were wonderful years as well, as she fulfilled God's plan for her life and with joy lived out her "divine calling."

• TALKING IT OVER •

---

1. REVIEW IN A GROUP.   *10 minutes*
   Review the three incidents the Bible gives us about Miriam:
   ☐ Exodus 2:1-8
   ☐ Exodus 15:20-21
   ☐ Numbers 12:1-16
   Choose one of these incidents and share:
   ☐ The lesson you learned
   ☐ A promise you can claim
   ☐ A warning to heed

---

2. STUDY ON YOUR OWN.   *10 minutes*
   Look up the following verses on pride and list your findings:
   ☐ Proverbs 8:13 – *is evil + God hates it*
   ☐ Proverbs 13:10 – *trouble*
   ☐ Proverbs 16:18 – *leads to destruction*
   ☐ Proverbs 29:23 – *degrades you*
   ☐ Daniel 4:37 – *God will set you right*

---

3. In groups of three discuss: *10 minutes*
   ☐ How do we discover our gifts?
   ☐ How do we exercise them?

•PRAYING IT THROUGH•

Suggested Times

---

1. (As a group) Praise God for:
   - ☐ Answered prayer
   - ☐ Creating and conditioning us for His plan and His purpose
   - ☐ Preserving us and our children in trouble
   - ☐ Being concerned when we suffer

8 minutes

---

2. (As a group) Pray for children like Moses who are abused, in danger, or unborn. Pray for leaders like Moses, Aaron, and Miriam.

7 minutes

---

3. (On your own) Pray for:
   - ☐ Yourself
   - ☐ Your family
   - ☐ Your work
   - ☐ Your world

5 minutes

•DIGGING DEEPER•

Huldah

Both Miriam and Huldah were prophetesses, a special and rare calling for a woman in the Old Testament. What outstanding characteristics did they jointly possess to have been entrusted with such a prized gift? (1 Corinthians 14:1) gift of prophecy

1. During the reign of King Josiah, Huldah was a prophetess. What can you surmise about the nation of Judah's spiritual climate during this time?

   2 Kings 21:19-22
   the King was evil

   2 Kings 22:13
   people weren't obeying God's word

   2 Kings 22:17
   worshiped idols

   2 Chronicles 33:21-25 amon was evil and he got assassinated

   2 Chronicles 34:3-7 Josiah destroyed all the idols and temples to other gods.

   2 Chronicles 34:8 Josiah sent Shaphan & Joah to repair the temple of God

   2 Chronicles 35:18 they celebrated passover

2. Read 2 Kings 22:14-20 and 2 Chronicles 34:22-33. Besides Huldah, what other prophet might have advised Josiah regarding the authenticity of the scroll? Jeremiah

   Why would the Lord choose a woman to fulfill this ministry in a male-oriented culture? God uses everyone

3. Consult a Bible help for the following definitions:

prophet — one who is a spokesman for God.

prophecy — messages from God and about the future

4. What must Huldah's character and lifestyle have exhibited in order to have been entrusted with this ministry?

Deuteronomy 13:1-5
served only God

Deuteronomy 18:20-22
shows the lifestyle of God

1 Peter 4:10-11
serve God with all strength

1 Peter 5-6
Humble yourself

5. Compare Huldah and Miriam. What did they have in common?
they both served God

6. Examine the content of Huldah's prophecy (cf. 2 Kings 22:14-20).

What did the Lord promise? (v. 16)
Bring disaster

What three accusations were made against Judah? (v. 17)
1 forsaken God
2 Burned incense to other gods [country?]
3 angered God with idols

In contrast, what three commendations did the Lord have for Josiah? (v. 19)
1 heart is responsive
2. humbled
3. Repented

What reward was Josiah given? (v. 20)

He will be buried in peace and he will not see the disaster

7. Huldah's ministry had a great influence on both Josiah and the nation of Judah. List the direct results of her prophecy.

2 Chronicles 34:30

they read the Book of the conederrt

2 Chronicles 34:31

renewed the conedent

2 Chronicles 34:33

removed all the idols Every on served God

2 Chronicles 35:1

Celebrated the Passover

8. Who has God placed under the authority of or within your sphere of influence? What effect could you have on their lives? What difference is your life making on theirs? What global impact could you make for Christ?

9. Josiah is considered to be among the few kings who brought about revival and reform. For what specifically does the chronicler remember him?

2 Chronicles 34:1-2

He was faithful to God

2 Chronicles 35:26

deeds of devotion

10. What memory are you leaving those you influence?

For Further Study

1. Memorize this list of the kings of both the Northern and the
   Southern Kingdoms:

Israel (Northern Kingdom)	*Judah (Southern Kingdom)*
Jeroboam	Rehoboam
Nadab	Abijam
Baasha	Asa
Elah	Jehoshaphat
Zimri	Jehoram
Omri	Ahaziah
Ahab	Athaliah
Ahaziah	Joash
Jehoram	Amaziah
Jehu	Azariah (Uzziah)
Jehoahaz	Jotham
Jehoash	Ahaz
Jeroboam II	Hezekiah
Zechariah	Manasseth
Shallum	Amon
Menahem	Josiah
Pekahiah	Jehoahaz
Pekah	Jehoiakim
Hoshea	Jehoiakin
	Zedekiah

2. Study other kings known for their godliness. Who influenced
   them for good?

•TOOL CHEST•
(A Suggested Optional Resource)

ELISABETH ELLIOT

Elisabeth Elliot was a missionary with her husband, Jim, to the Quichua and Auca Indians in Ecuador. It was their desire to bring the Word of God to peoples without Christ. Jim and four other missionaries were murdered by the Aucas in an attempt to make contact with this timid and hostile tribe. But Elisabeth's life and missionary work did not end with Jim's death. Betty Elliot and her baby daughter, Valerie, continued the work she and her husband had begun. God gave her a privilege similar to that which He gave Huldah. In time, the Aucas opened their hearts to the Lord Jesus, and Elisabeth was able to share God's precious Word with them. Betty Elliot is another woman who has changed her world through evangelism, missions, and her speaking and writing gifts. Her books include *Through Gates of Splendor, Passion and Purity, The Journals of Jim Elliot, Discipline: The Glad Surrender,* and *A Chance to Die.*

4

Changing Her World Through Faith
(Rahab)

•FOOD FOR THOUGHT•

There's a scarlet thread that runs through Scripture from Genesis to Revelation. It begins in Genesis 3:15 when God promises fallen man redemption, winds its way to the cross of Christ, and continues on until it stops in heaven at the very throne of the Lamb. Here and there throughout the Bible, a man or a woman hangs a scarlet thread out of the window of his or her life, saying in effect, "This symbolizes my identification with a Saviour." Rahab was such a person.

Rahab lived in the days of Joshua. God had told Joshua to take the Promised Land, drive out the Canaanites, and utterly destroy their cities. Rahab lived in Jericho, one of those Canaanite towns. Joshua dispatched two spies to survey the opposition. They came to Rahab's town and entered her house which was built on the city wall.

Some say she was an innkeeper; others indicate she was a prostitute. One way or another, the spies ended up with Rahab! The king of Jericho heard about them and told Rahab to deliver them up. Instead, she bravely hid them and sent the king's soldiers on a wild goose chase. She asked the spies to spare her family's lives when they took the city, and they promised her that they would if she kept her council and hung a scarlet thread in the window. She did. When Joshua came, she and her family were the only ones saved.

Rahab was an "outside inside" person. To look at her outside appearance, you wouldn't dream she was altogether another person inside. She was a hapless, helpless, hopeless girl, but she put on a very good facade living a flamboyant public life. Tradition has it she was *hapless* because she became a prostitute at the age of 10. A rare beauty, the Jewish rabbis said. She was *helpless* in her present distress, as according to her own testimony, her "heart melted and she had no more courage because of the coming attack" of the Israelites (Josh. 2:11). She felt *hopeless* because of her future prospects, saying to the spies, "I know that the Lord has given this land to you" (Josh. 2:9). And the land included her land, her house, her family, her very life!

Maybe you are like Rahab in the sense that you are aching on the inside because of a hapless past, a critical present, and a bleak future, but no one would ever guess because of the outside "front" you've managed to put on.

Rahab may well have become a worthless, valueless person in other people's eyes, but not in the eyes of God. She certainly reacts with unscrupulous haste as she lies to her king and becomes part of a conspiracy that resulted in the destruction of her whole city, but God doesn't look on the outside, but on the inside!

Today many women feel worthless and valueless and may have compromised their values to survive the abuse and indignities they have suffered, but all the time I believe women's hearts are crying out, "What I am on the *outside* has nothing whatsoever to do with who I really want to be on the *inside!*" However worthless you feel you are, you were worth the Son of God's life given on your behalf. You are of great eternal value in His eyes!

We must be careful not to evaluate people by appearances. God looks on the heart and we must ask Him to help us to see "inside." The "outside" too! God reminded Samuel of this when he looked at Eliab's height, looks, age, and experience, and was sure he must be the Lord's anointed, when all the time God was watching a smaller, younger, inexperienced boy called David with a great big heart for Him! (1 Sam. 16:6-12) So what did God see as He looked right "inside" Rahab?

He saw a seeker, who if given half a chance would become a fervent follower of Yahweh. He saw she believed that He was God in heaven above and on earth below (Josh. 2:11). She believed He was visible (Hadn't He dried up the Red Sea for His people?) and viable, a present, active God. What's more, she believed He was valuable, worth risking everything for, worth worshiping and cherishing.

The spies offered her salvation (which she accepted) and kept their promise to spare her and all in her house when judgment came to Jericho.

Then Rahab became an "inside outside" person! God saw her heart, met her need, forgave her sin, and turned her inside out! Now her outside matched her inside! God had seen the person she longed to be and began to change her into His image. He delivered her out of judgment and death and deposited her in a whole new wonderful world. He gave her a new family and a new future. Rabbinical tradition tells us that she became Joshua's wife and eight priests and prophets including Jeremiah were her progenies! But the Bible tells us she became Salmon's wife and the mother of Boaz, who married Ruth. She is certainly counted as a woman of faith (Heb. 11:31) and good works (James 2:25). Above all, her name appears in the genealogy of Christ Himself (Matt. 1:5), a testimony of the new direction her life took.

Our salvation mirrors Rahab's experience. Faced with rightful ruin because our sin offends a Holy God, the God of grace offers us the scarlet thread wet with the blood of His sacrifice. Like Rahab, we must choose to appropriate His offer of forgiveness and display our allegiance in the window of our lives. Then we need to become an "inside outside person." We must behave what we believe. We will need to make good choices concerning life partners, lifestyles, and directions. Then we will find ourselves inextricably connected with Christ and His cause and be counted women of faith and good works. God can change anyone. Has He changed us?

The Scarlet Thread

I've been where Rahab's been—
an outside inside person,
wondering what it would be like
to be changed internally into an inside outside one!

One of God's "spies" told me about the
scarlet thread.
I tied it in the window of my soul.
God will see it, I believe, and spare me...

I'll take it in my hands when
I meet Jesus.
I'll lay it at
His feet!
I know He'll pick it up,
weave it into a crown,
and place it on my head.

How proud I'll be to wear it.
He'll wear one too.

But His will have thorns all around.

My scarlet thread won't have thorns.
I need to remember that!

•TALKING IT OVER•

1. STUDY JOSHUA 2.　　　　　　　　　　　　　　　　*10 minutes*
   ☐ What does the scarlet thread represent?
   Read the genealogy in Matthew 1.
   ☐ What other names in this list are a surprise?
   Why?
   ☐ What does Rahab's story teach you about:
   God?
   Joshua?
   The spies?
   Rahab?
   Her family?

2. USE YOUR IMAGINATION.　　　　　　　　　　　　*10 minutes*
   Imagine you are Rahab.
   ☐ Would you find it hard to believe? Why?
   Imagine you are spies.
   ☐ What do you think they were tempted to do?
   Imagine you are Rahab's family.
   ☐ What would they be thinking?

3. SHARE.　　　　　　　　　　　　　　　　　　　　*10 minutes*
   Have you been an Outside Inside person? Have you
   become an Inside Outside one?

• PRAYING IT THROUGH •

*Suggested
Times*

1. (On your own) Pray for people who:
   □ Appear to have no inner need
   □ Need to hang "the scarlet thread" in their lives
   □ Are in your family who won't believe the truth

   8 minutes

2. (As a group) Read Hebrews 11:31 and meditate on why Rahab is mentioned in this chapter. Praise God *your* name is in God's book. (If you are not sure it is, ask God to write it in right now!)

   7 minutes

3. (In twos) Pray about "Rahabs" who have been delivered from judgment but are not "behaving their beliefs." Pray for the Jerichos of this world, doomed unless God has mercy and the people turn to Him.

   5 minutes

•DIGGING DEEPER•

Lydia

Rahab and Lydia were both first generation believers. Neither had a Christian heritage to lean upon. Both took great risks to embrace their newfound faith. What encouragement can you draw from their lives?

1. A captivating quality often accompanies a new convert to Christianity. Recall someone who fits this description. Is there anything striking to you about them?

2. Read Acts 16:11-15, 40. Draw a map below charting Paul's travels in this passage. What continent is Paul taking the Gospel to for the first time? *Macedonica*

3. When doing thorough Bible study we should always attend to any changes in geography. Using a Bible dictionary, look up the following locations and take notes of significant details in their descriptions.

   Troas - *name of a city + a region.*

   Somothrace - *island*

   Neapolis - *town in the N shore of the Agean Sea*

   Philippi - *the position dominated road system of northern Greece*

Macedonia — *Greek Kingdom + Roman*
Providence
Thyatira — *boundary of Lydia + Mysia*

4. What is unusual regarding where Paul spent this particular Sabbath in contrast to other Sabbaths during his missionary journeys? (Acts 13:5, 14, 42-44; 14:1; 17:1-4, 10, 16-17; 18:1-4, 19)

They spent it in the synagogue + taught God's word.

16:B What did Paul and his companions expect to find by the river and why? *went to the river — place of prayer*

5. What does this passage reveal about European women in general during the first century A.D.? *interested in spiritual stuff*

6. What does it tell us specifically about Lydia?

Her vocation — *dealer in purple cloth*

Her spiritual condition — *God opened her heart*

Her generous spirit — *offered her home*

Her financial status — *probably wealthy*

7. What evidence did Lydia demonstrate of her newfound faith in the Lord Jesus? *invited Paul to stay with them. family got baptized*

52

8. What changes might you expect to see in Lydia's business practice, household, lifestyle, and friendships as a result of her conversion?

   she would put God first + be an example to others

9. What honor was given to Lydia that she is still known for 2,000 years later?

   Help start Church

10. Give four ways Lydia and Rahab are alike.

    1. Offered her home
    2. Opened to God
    3. at first lived ungodly lives
    4. examples

11. Are there any women entrepreneurs in your life who in your estimation are unlikely (such as Rahab) or likely (such as Lydia) Christian candidates? Write their names below and pray:

    For an opportunity to befriend them
    For an opportunity to share with them the message of salvation
    For the Lord to open their hearts as He did Lydia's
    For them to have a tremendous righteous influence in the marketplace

12. What can Lydia teach us about:

    Serving missionaries? *providing for them*

    Keeping an "open door" policy at home? *Offering our homes*

    Generosity? *helping them*
    helping

    Being unashamed of the Gospel?
    taught others

Not allowing our professions to dictate our spirituality?

13. How can you and your family begin today to have a positive influence for Christ in your neighborhood, marketplace, and community?

For Further Study
1. In the verses listed below, what did Jesus indicate were the true evidences of Christian belief and conversion?

   John 14:12
   John 14:15, 23
   John 15:5
   John 15:17
   John 15:19
   John 16:15

2. Read Philippians 1:1-11. What does Paul commend the worshipers at Philippi for and how does he pray for them?

•TOOL CHEST•
(A Suggested Optional Resource)

DALE HANSON BOURKE
Everyday Miracles: Holy Moments in a Mother's Life by Dale Hanson Bourke is a glimpse into a mother's heart yearning for her children to know Christ and the reality of a life in Christ. What Dale so marvelously grasps for her reader is the mystery of a *child* teaching his mother spiritual truths. Dale is a woman influencing mothers and the marketplace by her striving for excellence. Like Lydia, she is an entrepreneur. Among her outstanding accomplishments, she is senior editor of *Today's Christian Woman* and president of Publishing Directions, Inc. Dale is an articulate communicator and has also authored *You Can Make Your Dreams Come True.*

5

Changing Her World Through Strength
(Deborah)

•FOOD FOR THOUGHT•

This is the story of Honeybee and Thunderbolt—otherwise known as Deborah and Barak. Joshua was dead, the tribes of Israel though loosely organized were scattered, demoralized, and experiencing anything but the blessing they had anticipated when they entered Canaan.

God had revealed Himself to all mankind from the time of Adam to the Flood, but after the men He made rejected Him continually, He decided to execute His great plan of redemption through one people whose father was Abraham. After this, the benefits would be taken back to the whole world again.

Part of the plan was to increase this nation numerically and give it a special place in which to live—the land of Canaan. A principal feature of this plan was that the Lord would be this nation's Supreme Ruler, making the final decisions for the people. Unlike any other nation, God would be King. This would call for the complete obedience of every individual.

There were to be no civil officials, though certain people would hold relative authority. There would be priests, prophets, prophetesses, and judges. The priests would have an oral teaching ministry, presenting sacrifices to model the idea of substitution for sin, and they would use the Urim and Thummim (sacred lots) to discern God's will.

The civil elders would be older, wiser people who would judge murders, hear family disputes, and settle controversy in the city gates. The prophets would have no government function, but they would bring a message from God to motivate and encourage.

When God's people rejected God's government, He raised up judges, fourteen in all, for the emergency situations that arose because of the people's disobedience. Deborah was one of these. She was also a prophetess, the only judge so gifted. She was also a woman!

Deborah held court under the palm tree and listened with great compassion to the stories of the oppression of the Israelites by Jabin, king of the Canaanites and Sisera, his commander. The people told Deborah their troubles, and God told her to select Barak to deliver them. Deborah called for him and he responded, but said he wouldn't do it without her. She responded by rebuking him for his timidity, but encouraged him to go ahead in the Lord's strength. Barak chased Jabin's army back home, though it was Jael, a Kenite woman, that nailed Sisera (literally finishing him off with a tent peg through his head!), thus fulfilling Deborah's prophecy about the matter (Jud. 5:26).

Deborah was many things. Mostly she was a warrior of the Lord and a fighter. Are we? First, we need to realize there is a battle going on, a war to be won. I remember as a little girl hearing the news that Germany had invaded Poland. I asked my mother what that meant. "We are at war," she replied simply. We were!

The forces of evil have invaded the forces of good in our world today. We are at war. It is God's war. Souls are at stake. Christ is our Commander and we men and women are His soldiers.

When Joshua first entered the Promised Land, he was met by the angel of the Lord. "Whose side are you on?" he asked the angel, amazed at the sight of this incredible being with his gleaming sword (Josh. 5:13). In essence the angel of the Lord replied, "I am the Captain of the Lord's army. I haven't come to take sides; I've come to take over!" He came to tell Joshua that we must fight God's battles, but He will direct us in the fight. Deborah encouraged Barak to remember this (Jud. 4:6; 5:23). So the war we fight against evil is the Lord's, Christ is our commander and we are His soldiers.

God has an Air Force—unseen ranks in the heavenlies (Jud. 5:20; Eph. 6:12), but He also has land forces—us. This vast army is made up of both men and women. God uses women to fight His battles as surely as He uses men.

God used Deborah—not because Barak didn't get his act together—rather He chose to use her one way and Barak another. God doesn't only use a woman when He can't find a man, but when He can find a man as well. On occasions, He uses women to do what men usually do! No one else but God's Honeybee could sting Barak, who had shot his bolt, into renewal and action! We need each other.

Deborah and Barak were a powerful combination once both were being all that God had called and gifted them to be.

Make no mistake about it, today the opposition is as fierce as in those days. Barak saw 900 iron chariots ranged against him and knew the Canaanites had stripped the Israelites of their weapons, but Deborah reminded him that God was on their side (Jud. 4:14). Both Elijah and Elisha had seen the fiery horses and chariots that surrounded God's warriors (2 Kings 2:11; 6:16-17). Barak came to experience the truth of Elisha's words, "Those who are with us are more than those who are with them" (2 Kings 6:16). So must we!

Our world is waiting for God's people to stop going AWOL and get back to the battlefield. We can be God's "Honeybees" helping "Thunderbolt" to get into the fray. We must not loose our strength. We need to be aware of our world, hold court under our own particular palm trees, and be wise women, respecting the enemies' strength, but counting on the Captain of the Lord of Hosts to fight with us, for us, and through us. We must have compassion and be a true mother in Israel as Deborah was—caring for people as if they are our very own. Then we will see Jabin and Sisera overcome, and we will have done our bit to change our world!

•TALKING IT OVER•

*Suggested
Times*

---

1. REVIEW.

Review what the following did in Israel's corporate life:

☐ Priests
☐ Prophets
☐ Elders
☐ Judges

10 minutes

---

2. READ.

Read Deborah's song in Judges 5.

☐ Who stayed home?
☐ Why did they stay home?
☐ What did Deborah think about them?
☐ How can we apply this today?

10 minutes

---

3. RECOUNT.

Recount what this story teaches you about:

☐ God
☐ Christ
☐ Barak
☐ Deborah
☐ Jabin
☐ Sisera
☐ Jael
☐ Yourself

10 minutes

•PRAYING IT THROUGH•

Suggested Times

---

1. (As a group) Praise God for:
   - ☐ Being the God of battles
   - ☐ Bothering to fight for our souls
   - ☐ Sending us a Captain
   - ☐ Strengthening our hands to war

5 minutes

---

2. (On your own) Pray for the church in disarray and for soldiers who are AWOL or timid like Barak.

5 minutes

---

3. (As a group) Pray for "Deborahs" to be raised up for:
   - ☐ The church
   - ☐ Missions
   - ☐ The community
   - ☐ Politics
   - ☐ Families

5 minutes

---

4. (In twos) Pray for cooperation between men and women and not competition as demonstrated by Deborah and Barak. Pray about your part in God's war and that the war will be won.

5 minutes

•DIGGING DEEPER•

Anna

Anna resembles Deborah in several ways. Her reputation as both prophetess and one who had dedicated her life to God's service reveal her great *wisdom*. She was also a *warrior*. A woman who fought her battle with prayer and fasting.

1. Luke introduces Anna in Luke 2:36-38. Read his account and then reread it within its surrounding context. Why do you think Luke included this story of Anna in his birth narrative? What is its relationship to Luke 2:21-35 and Luke 2:39-40? Check your answer with the book *Daughters of the Church*, suggested in the *Tool Chest* of chapter 1. To give an example of some ways God uses women.

2. Names in the Bible often have special significance. Look up Anna and Phanuel in a Bible dictionary. How do these names lend credibility to Luke's record of Christ's birth?

    Anna - grace

    Phanuel - face of God

3. Prophecy is the God-given gift of foretelling and forthtelling. To foretell, the prophet must have knowledge of an event before it happens. To forthtell is to serve as God's spokesman or spokeswoman in proclaiming the Lord's instruction, correction, or judgment to others. How did Anna fulfill both of these functions?

    She was messager for Godtelling people what he was going to do

4. How long had Anna been widowed? How had she spent her widowhood? What example is she to those of us who may one day find ourselves in her position as widows or widowers?

    ~50-55 years, fasting + praying we can trust in God to take care of us.

5. How does Anna's life personify Paul's advice to widows in 1 Timothy 5:3-16?

    She prayed day + night and put God first

6. How did Anna fulfill her "gift and calling"?

   She shared the Gospel

7. The Lord chose to use Anna to fulfill a unique and privileged ministry. How did she prepare herself to be His instrument?

   praying + giving thanks

8. What do the Scriptures teach about fasting (consult a concordance)? *Do it with the right motive + in secret + to deny the physical need*

9. What fruit of the Spirit must Anna have cultivated to have spent a life in fasting and prayer? (cf. Gal. 5:23; 1 Thes. 5:6, 8; 1 Tim. 3:2; Titus 1:8; 2:2, 5-6, 12; 1 Peter 1:13; 4:7; 5:8; 2 Peter 1:6) What Christian qualities are worth your life investment?

   love, peace, patience, goodness, faithfulness, self-control, joy, kindness

10. What two verbs describe Anna's Christian service in verse 38?

    gave, spoke

11. Anna is reputed for having been the first female to proclaim the good news of Jesus Christ, His incarnation and redemption. Like Deborah she was . . .

    a prophetess
    a (prayer) warrior of the Lord
    a wise woman
    a woman who played her part in God's plan
    a woman who dared to do her bit to change her world (as the first missionary)

    Choose one of the designations that you need to cultivate and pray daily this week that the Holy Spirit would conform you to Christ's image in the particular area of concern to you.

For Further Study
1. Ask a known "prayer warrior" in your church to be your mentor for one year, focusing on the area of prayer.
2. Investigate how the widows of your church are being cared for. If this ministry is lacking in any biblical manner, try to improve it.
3. Examine Dr. Leon Wood's *The Prophets of Israel* (Baker) or Abraham Heschel's two volume work, *The Prophets*, for a deeper understanding of the definition of prophecy and the role the prophet fulfilled.

•TOOL CHEST•
(A Suggested Optional Resource)

THE GENERAL WAS A LADY

The General Was a Lady by Margaret Troutt is the biography of Evangeline Booth. Eva was the daughter of William and Catherine Booth, founders of the Salvation Army. Their spiritual daughter served as director of the Salvation Army both in Canada and the United States and eventually became the Salvation Army's General, which is the top position of this worldwide organization dedicated to evangelism and social ministry. She served her Lord with passion and determination, facing each obstacle with a solution orientation often employing unconventional methods. Eva was a soldier of Christ and changed her world by aggressively tackling Satan's opposition. Like Deborah, she was a defensive player in God's army.

Eva lived among the poor and became known as the White Angel of the Slums. A strong opponent of drink, she helped shut down pubs and taverns. She loved the poor and the working people and helped establish Goodwill Centers to meet their needs.

Her love for children and orphans shall never be forgotten. A single woman, she adopted four children. In 1938 she launched the Torchbearers, an international youth movement.

Preaching the Gospel was the love of her life and she did so with vigor well into her eighties. She held thousands spellbound with her oratory skills and proclaimed God's Word to many renowned audiences. Evangeline Booth was one of the most outstanding women of this last century and devoted her life to the interest of Christ and His battles.

6

Changing Her World Through Love
(Ruth)

•FOOD FOR THOUGHT•

Eve changed her world by sinning, Sarah by her meek and quiet spirit, Miriam by her gifts, and Rahab by her faith in Jehovah. Deborah changed her world by fighting the Lord's battles, and Ruth changed hers by love.

Ruth's world was a sad world, a world of good-byes. She said good-bye to her own people in order to travel with her mother-in-law to her native Bethlehem, to her husband on his deathbed, and to her sister-in-law, who changed her mind about accompanying them to Israel. Her world was a world of sexual perversion and spiritual darkness, for she was a Moabitess living among a people who sacrificed their children to their gods by fire, and engaged in sexual orgies in their religious festivals. Ruth's world surely needed changing, and the only thing that could change it was love!

Love is as strong as death. It moves empires, wins wars, dethrones despots, and reduces violent men to tears. Human love does all these things—so how much more will the love of God change our world? God's love is concerned always with the "others'" well-being, irrespective of the cost, and Ruth's story shows us this sort of love in action!

Ruth's name means "friendship." Proverbs says, "A friend loves at all times," and Ruth certainly lived and loved up to her name. In the last chapter of the Book of Ruth, the women of Bethlehem are talking about Ruth. They are commenting to Naomi how very much Ruth loves her. "Why," they say, "your daughter-in-law, who loves you, is better to you than seven sons." Seven was a number associated with perfection, so in essence the women were saying Ruth's love was worth the love of seven perfect sons! Considering the revered place of sons in the society of the day, this was high praise!

Paul gives a description of God's love in 1 Corinthians 13:4-7, finishing by saying, "Love never fails!" (1 Cor. 13:8) As we look at the Book of Ruth, we can see how every aspect of this quality love can be seen in her actions.

"Love is patient and kind," says Paul. One definition of patience is, "love waiting out suffering." Ruth was married to Mahlon, Orpah to Killion—both Naomi's boys. The boys' names mean "sickness" and "pining" which give a hint of their delicate constitution. Ten years after their father Elimelech's death in the land of Moab, both sons died as well, so Ruth must have had plenty of opportunity to practice loving patience. Chronically sick people are not always easy to live with and not everyone dies well.

Kindness is the active part of patience. Patience is *being* good, while kindness is *doing* good, and Ruth showed much love in her many practical deeds of kindness. Three times in the narrative Ruth is commended for her kindness. Everyone is talking about it—after all, there was so little kindness in her cold world. In Ruth 1:8 Naomi says, "May the Lord show kindness to you as you have shown to your dead husband and to me." Boaz commends her not only for her kindness to Naomi, but also to himself! (2:11; 3:10)

Love, says Paul, doesn't envy and isn't proud. Ruth returned with Naomi to live among the Israelites. The women were poor, even though both of them had known better times. It must have taken humility for Ruth to take the place of a servant and seek employment gleaning in the fields in order to put bread on the table. Naomi had a near relative, Boaz, whose responsibility it was to marry Naomi. Ruth could have envied her mother-in-law, coveting the handsome older man of "good-standing" for herself. But love doesn't envy and it isn't proud. You don't change your world that way!

Paul tells us love isn't self-seeking, neither is it easily angered. Ruth surely noticed how many people *could* have helped them when they first came home to Bethlehem. Boaz wasn't the only near relative around apparently, and she could have become angry with Naomi for not pulling her weight and helping her in the fields. Not only could she have gotten mad at Boaz and Naomi, but she could easily have lost it with God as well! Losing your temper, however, doesn't solve anything—rather the reverse—love knows that! Doesn't the Scripture say, "The wrath of man doesn't work the righteousness of God"?

Paul says that love keeps no record of wrongs. That it forgets, quickly, refusing to gossip about people's misdoings, rejoicing rather in the truth. Ruth had plenty of opportunity to gossip about her new neighbors, but she kept her peace when Boaz told her to (3:14). Of course, her secret was her new love of Jehovah, "Under whose wings" she had come to take refuge (2:12). Love *always* trusts, says Paul. Corrie ten Boom used to say, "Don't wrestle—nestle!" Ruth nestled under God's wings and found in His love her security and reward, despite her precarious situation.

'Love," says the apostle, "never gives up!" Love never fails to love, and neither did Ruth. She married Boaz, for Naomi, changed by her daughter-in-law's loving friendship, yielded her right to Boaz in Ruth's favor. A child was born called Obed, which means "worship," and Naomi took him in her arms and cared for him.

True love doesn't stop loving when the hard times hit and it doesn't stop loving when the sun comes out either! Love commits itself to loving whatever, whenever, if ever anyone loves him back! "Where you go I will go," sings love. "Where you live, I will live. Where you die, I will die" (1:16-17). When we like Ruth are stead-fastly determined to love people with God's love in such a fashion, we'll change our world!

•TALKING IT OVER•

---

1. READ RUTH 1.   *10 minutes*
   - [ ] Why do you think Naomi thought God was punishing her? *the death of her husband & sons*
   - [ ] Do people in difficult situations today feel like that? *yes*

---

2. READ RUTH 2.   *5 minutes*
   God is in this chapter. Can you see His shadow?
   Where? *In Boaz, the kindness he showed*

---

3. READ RUTH 3.   *5 minutes*
   Giving reasons from the text, what do you think the following were thinking?
   - [ ] Boaz
   - [ ] Ruth
   - [ ] The servant girls
   - [ ] The reapers

---

4. READ RUTH 4.   *10 minutes*
   How did God provide for:
   - [ ] Naomi?
   - [ ] Ruth? *Husband*
   - [ ] Boaz? *Wife*
   - [ ] Obed?
   How is God providing for you?

•PRAYING IT THROUGH•

*Suggested
Times*

1. (As a group) Read 1 Corinthians 13:4-7. Praise God for this portrait of love.

    4 minutes

2. (On your own) Pray prayers of repentance over some aspect of these verses. (e.g., "Forgive me, Lord, I have held a grudge against my sister—")

    4 minutes

3. (On your own) Pray prayers of petition that one particular needed aspect of love will be shown in your life. (e.g., "Lord, help me to be patient with ————.")

    7 minutes

4. (As a group) Pray for the Naomis you know, the Ruths, the Orpahs.

    5 minutes

•DIGGING DEEPER•

Mary of Bethany
Ruth and Mary were ordinary, yet exceptional women who knew the meaning of sacrificial love. Each in her own manner was willing to pay the price of humiliation for the sake of love. Are we?

1. Read John 12:1-8. What event took place in John 11 that might explain why "a dinner was given in Jesus' honor"? (12:2)

   Jesus raised Lazarus from the dead

2. How did Martha and Mary each show their gratitude to Jesus? (12:2-3) Martha served dinner + Mary washed his feet with perfume

3. Place yourself in Mary's position. What feelings would you experience as you anointed Jesus' feet? Honor

4. Mary's act of devotion was prompted by Jesus' act of compassion (cf. 11:33, 35, 38ff). Both were practical demonstrations of love and fulfilled what biblical principles? (cf. James 1:22; John 13:34-35; 1 John 3:18; 4:7) love one another

5. Mary's gift was expensive. What costs did she incur? How is she similar to Ruth? a year's wage made sacrifices

6. Judas accused Mary of poor stewardship. Assuming John 12:1-8 and Mark 14:1-10 describe the same incident, what comments does Jesus make in defense of Mary? (Mark 14:6, 8)

   Always have the poor but not always him

72

7. Jesus, aware of Judas' true motives (John 12:6), reminded the latter that he would have ample opportunity to care for the poor if he was honestly concerned about their welfare. Consider Mary and Judas, i.e., their motives and values.

8. What contrast is made between Jesus and Lazarus in John 11:38-44 and John 12:1-8?

   John 11 - Jesus did Lazarus a favor
   John 12 - Lazarus did Jesus a favor

9. Why do Christians refer to this story as Jesus' anointing? What was significant to Jesus in this event? (Mark 14:8; John, 11:7)

   It was preparing Jesus for is burial

10. In Mark 14:9, Jesus memorializes Mary. Make a list of what you will remember her for from your study. Why does Jesus associate Mary with the proclamation of the Gospel?

    She did all she could for Jesus

11. Review the accounts from Scripture of Mary's life: Mark 14:1-10; Luke 10:38-41; John 11; 12:1-8. Notice that Mary is a silent figure. She speaks but once repeating Martha's words of anguish. She is remembered for what she did, not for what she said. Apply the lessons Mary's life teaches by reflecting on one of these questions.

    What generally consumes your thought life? Money? Greed? Devotion? Service?

    Mary gave to Jesus what she could; have you?

    What beautiful thing have you done to/for the Lord?

    Have you given Jesus something of equal value to a year's income?

Mary abandoned her reputation to love, serve, and worship her Lord. Are you holding back from doing the same? Do you take personal risks to practically demonstrate your love for others?

For Further Study
1. Where does Jesus' triumphal entry occur in relation to His anointing in Mark and in John? Why this difference?
2. How often is the command to love one another given in all of John's writings? Why does he place such emphasis on love?

•TOOL CHEST•
(A Suggested Optional Resource)

AMY CARMICHAEL

Amy Carmichael served her Lord as a single missionary in southern India at the turn of the century. Although she never married she was known as "Amma," or mother to hundreds of Indian children. Amy began her mission work as a gifted itinerant evangelist, but soon God broke her heart over the babies raised in the Hindu temples. Her love for Christ and the lost was practically demonstrated as she literally built an orphanage for the little ones God brought to her. Over the years the work grew from caring practically and spiritually for a handful of children to a Fellowship housing nearly a thousand. She risked her life and reputation more than once for the salvation and protection of others. Amy certainly fought to change her world. A gifted writer, she authored many books filled with the stories of God's work and wonders in India. One of her biographers concludes:

> Ask her "children," ask the members of the Fellowship, what most impressed them about Amma, and the reply never varies. "It was her love." "I was thinking this morning," she wrote to a member of the Fellowship in 1939, "Of what I would say if I had to put what I want each of you seniors to do for the others into two sentences. Love them dearly. Hold them to the Highest. I think I would say." And that is what she did. She loved with infinite tenderness, but it was not a love that weakened. No—it held her family to the highest. I truly believe that in none of His disciples in this century was our Lord's prayer, "that the love wherewith Thou hast loved Me may be in them," more fully answered than in Amy Carmichael (Houghton, pp. xiv-xv).

Books about Amy include: *Amy Carmichael of Dohnavur* by Frank Houghton, Christian Literature Crusade, Pennsylvania, 1973; *A Chance to Die: the Life and Legacy of Amy Carmichael* by Elisabeth Elliot, Fleming H. Revell Company, Old Tappan, New Jersey, 1987.
Books authored by Amy include:

Candles in the Dark (Christian Literature Crusade)
Edges of His Ways (Christian Literature Crusade)
Figures of the True (Christian Literature Crusade)
God's Missionary (Christian Literature Crusade)
Gold by Moonlight (Christian Literature Crusade)
His Thoughts Said (Christian Literature Crusade)

If (Zondervan Publishing House)
Learning of God (Christian Literature Crusade)
Mimosa (Christian Literature Crusade)
Rose From Brier (Christian Literature Crusade)
Thou Givest . . . They Gather (Christian Literature Crusade)
Towards Jerusalem (Christian Literature Crusade)
Whispers of His Power (Fleming H. Revell)

7

Changing Her World Through Faithfulness
(Abigail)

• FOOD FOR THOUGHT •

Abigail lived in an angry world. She was married to a difficult man, a drunk and evil man. She must have learned to cope with him daily. The way she handled him changed her world. We may not all be married to difficult men, but most of us experience or face anger frequently. Let's see what Abigail can teach us.

The background to Abigail's story is colorful and dangerous. Saul has hired David, becomes insanely jealous of him, and tries to kill him. David runs for his life and collects a whole crew of distressed, discontented debtors around him. He shapes them into a formidable fighting force. He then hides in caves and forests and becomes a sort of ancient Robin Hood to the people in isolated villages. Saul continues to hunt him down, and David, refusing to retaliate, finds himself trapped. God protects him and he spares Saul's life twice when it is in his power to kill him. Samuel dies and Israel mourns their prophet priest, which gives David a little respite, but once the period of national mourning is over, David is pursued relentlessly again.

Hiding in the rugged countryside, David and his men find themselves rubbing shoulders with a wealthy man's shepherds. They treat the herdsmen kindly, protecting them, and are careful not to steal their animals. When sheepshearing time comes along, David sends his servants to Nabal (the wealthy man) to ask for remuneration in the form of food and supplies. Nabal curses and insults the men and sends them off empty-handed. David gets mad! He decides to get even and his 400 men take off vowing to exterminate Nabal's family. Enter Abigail.

Abigail is married to Nabal! Now there's an interesting thing! How did that happen? How did two such opposite people ever get married in the first place? Well, probably it was an arranged marriage! The greater mystery to me is how we end up with Nabals and Abigails married today when it is a matter of choice!

Nabal's name means "son of the devil"! I can't imagine what sort of mother would choose such a name for her baby, but Abigail says that by the time he was grown, his name matched his nature! (1 Sam. 25:25) The historian tells us he was wealthy, self-indulgent, surly, churlish, a boor, mean, and miserly. He also had a drinking problem. Even his own servants said, "no one can talk to him," so I think we can see that Abigail had her hands full!

In stark contrast, Abigail is described as a wise woman, very intelligent, approachable, courageous, tactful, a self-controlled lady! Now if Abigail lived at the end of the 20th century, it probably wouldn't take her long to remove her wedding band. In her day it was the Nabals who had the power to divorce the Abigails, not the other way around, so she was left with no alternative but to live as well as she could in a bad marriage. How then did she cope?

First, she nurtured her relationship with God. As she said in verse 26, she believed Yahweh lived, was Judge of all men, and she was answerable to Him (v. 30). We are, after all, only responsible for our own actions and not the actions of other people! She was committed to Nabal and she was committed to God and until He intervened or Nabal took action, she got on with it!

Second, she was a concerned and compassionate woman. Maybe she loved Nabal. Anyway, she certainly was concerned enough to try and save his life by risking her own.

Third, she was clean! She decided she wasn't going to cheat! Sometimes if women decide to stay in a difficult relationship, they think they have the right to cheat! Some say it's the only way they can find the power to stay put.

Abigail had a good opportunity to cheat on Nabal. She was, I'm sure, woman enough to see the gleam in David's eye when she met him, yet David respected her. It would have been very easy for Abigail to offer herself to David along with the raisin cakes she had brought as a gift! Most of us women know how to say, "I'm available and reachable," but we don't say it in words or body language if we have clean hearts before the Lord.

Lastly, Abigail was controlled. She did not allow herself to retaliate and say, "It's all right to be angry. I deserve to be treated better. Let him have it, David. Here you go, have a map. Our house is the first one on the right as you come into the village—and give him one for me!" Getting revenge isn't going to solve a bad marriage. Yes, it's all right to be angry, but what we do with our anger makes the difference.

Abigail was as controlled with Nabal as she had been with David. Returning home and finding her husband very drunk, she waited till morning to tell him she had gone to David to plead for his life. The news sobered Nabal in a hurry. In fact, he suffered a stroke, and the Lord took his life 10 days later! At this, David sent for Abigail and she became *his* wife! How fortunate David was. Abigail had coped beautifully with David already, and no doubt enriched his life immeasurably in the following years.

So how do we live with other people's anger? Speak softly, for a "soft answer turns away wrath." Speak sweetly. Abigail looked for some way she could agree with David's reason for his anger and found it. Speak spiritual words of encouragement. "God has put you in His wallet," she told David! "You are precious to him. Don't let your anger spoil your record with the Almighty." David had spared Saul's life, yet was about to shed innocent blood (all Nabal's household). Abigail was able to remind him of his relationship with God who would vindicate him!

I am certainly not advocating women stay in abusive situations. But if a difficult relationship is not dangerous, a commitment to our Maker, our marriage, and the man we have married for better and for worse may result in God working in and through us to change our world. Please, God, may we be Abigails!

•TALKING IT OVER•

*Suggested
Times*

---

1. REVIEW.
   Tell the story of Abigail a sentence at a time. Go
   round the group till the story is finished.

   10 minutes

---

2. DESCRIBE.
   Describe the following as you see them in this
   story:
   ☐ Nabal
   ☐ Abigail
   ☐ David

   5 minutes

---

3. DISCUSS.
   Discuss the following questions.
   ☐ Is incompatibility a good reason for divorce?
   ☐ Did Abigail do the right or wrong thing by going
     behind Nabal's back?
   ☐ What sort of abusive behavior does Nabal ex-
     hibit?
   ☐ What do you think of the happy ending to the
     story?

   5 minutes

---

4. SHARE.
   Share in twos a need in each of your lives that has
   to do with anger. What one thing from this lesson
   will help you to cope?

   10 minutes

• PRAYING IT THROUGH •

Suggested Times

1. (As a group) Praise God for partners in difficult marriages intent on doing everything to save them. Pray for them and their difficult partners.

   4 minutes

2. (As a group) Praise God for your own families. Pray for them.

   4 minutes

3. (In twos) Pray for the victims of abusive situations — the Abigails and their children. Pray for happy endings to these dilemmas.

   7 minutes

4. (As a group) Pray for people coping with:
   ☐ Their own anger
   ☐ Other people's anger

   5 minutes

•DIGGING DEEPER•

The Woman of Samaria

Abigail and the woman of Samaria hardly seem likely candidates to be paired together. See if you can't find at least one similarity in their actions and/or attitudes.

1. Read John 4:1-42. Record your first impressions of Jesus and of the woman.

   the woman was seeking
   Jesus wanted to share the gospel
   with everyone, no matter who they were

2. These passages provide the background for the racial hatred between Jews and Samaritans. What indicators for this prejudice do you observe in them?

   2 Kings 17:21-41 *They treated God as just another idol*

   Ezra 4 *they did not want them to get another powerful king*

   Nehemiah 4 *They wanted to destroy the Jews*

   Consult a Bible dictionary for a deeper knowledge of the racial tension and take notes to share with your group. What examples exist today which are similar?

3. Describe Jesus' attitude toward Samaritans (cf. Luke 9:51-56; Luke 10:30-37; Luke 17:11-19). What do these references add to your impression of Jesus?

   That he was there for everyone
   no matter who they were

4. In John 4:27 the disciples are surprised that Jesus is speaking to a woman in public. Rabbinic law taught that a man should not address even his own wife in public. More severely, it condemned the public teaching of the words of the Law to women. What does

Jesus' conversation with the woman signify about His view of women? *Every one is equal*

5. What exchange is Jesus encouraging her to make in John 4:10-14?
living water for regular water

6. What does the Lord's knowledge of her past and present condition imply? (John 4:16-19) In what manner does He draw attention to her sin? *That he knows everything about us*

7. What privilege does Jesus give this woman? (4:25-26)
The knowledge that he is God

8. What evidence does she give of a changed life? (4:27ff)

9. Jesus changed this woman's life; what did she change in return? (4:39-42) *Many of the samaratean's lives in that town*

10. Give a parallel between Abigail and the woman at the well.
Both had a bad past and were willing to have a better future

11. Whose life have you changed since Christ changed yours? Have you shared your testimony with your hometown?

For Further Study
See William Barclay's treatment of the view of women in New Testament times in *The Daily Study Bible Series Gospel of John, I,* Revised Edition © 1975, Westminster Press: Philadelphia.

•TOOL CHEST•
(A Suggested Optional Resource)

CORRIE TEN BOOM

Corrie ten Boom lived a very quiet life with her family in Haarlem, Holland until she was middle-aged. It was then that God began to reveal the work He had prepared for her to do. During World War II Corrie and her family began to assist the Dutch resistance by hiding and smuggling Jews out of occupied Holland. They were motivated by the love of God and God's love for the sanctity of human life. Betrayed and caught, the ten Boom sisters were separated from their father and sent to the Nazi death camps. Corrie lost both her father and sister in the brutal camps. It was in a lice infested concentration camp that Corrie's faith was tried and found true. There she discovered God is enough and able to meet our every need.

After the war, Corrie tramped across the world literally on faith and prayer. She preached the transforming message of Jesus Christ and His love and forgiveness. She also authored numerous books about the same. Like the woman at the well, she did not let pride or prejudice hide her testimony of Christ's love and His offer of eternal life. *The Hiding Place, Tramp for the Lord,* and *The Five Silent Years of Corrie ten Boom* tell her life story.

8

Changing Her World Through Forgiveness
(Naaman's Little Maid)

•FOOD FOR THOUGHT•

Naaman was a great man with his master—but he was a leper. Leprosy was a terrible, incurable, debilitating, deadening, death-dealing malady that affected many, many people in biblical times. People were not always excluded from society, but since the disease was contagious if raw sores appeared in exposed parts of the body, the affected person would be separated from the community. Naaman was captain of the forces of the king of Syria, so apparently the disease had not advanced to the point of banishing him from the people.

Naaman, whose name means "delight," was "a great delight to his master," not only because he had led a successful rebellion and gained independence for his country from the rule of the king of Assyria, but because he was also an honorable man. He was a good soldier liked by his own men. It appears that God Himself had given him his greater victory. But despite the fact Naaman was a great man with his master and honorable in the eyes of his soldiers, he was still a leper. Though I'm sure he handled his personal battles as well as he handled his public ones, being brave didn't rid him of his leprosy.

Leprosy is a good picture of sin and its effects. The soul of man is deadened and destroyed by sin. It doesn't matter how well respected we are in the eyes of people, or how well we live our lives and conduct our affairs; it matters not if we are wonderfully brave about the hard things of life, because the deadening effects of this progressive disease of the soul will eventually end in death from God. There is, however, a cure.

Consider Naaman's story. During a raid into Israel's territory, the Syrians captured a little servant girl. We do not know her name or age, and actually we know very little about her at all, except that she served Naaman's mistress and apparently had faith in Israel's God. What is more, she shared her faith with her mistress and master. In doing so, she managed to change her world.

One thing we do learn about her, however, is that she had been able to overcome the trauma she had experienced as a teenager. Imagine guerillas bursting into your home and kidnapping you. Think of being that child, the terror and fear smothering you as you were rushed farther and farther away from the people that were part and parcel of your very life. This child—however old—must have been a specially gifted one, for she ended up in high places, chosen no doubt for her abilities and appearance. We don't know how long she had been in Naaman's household, but she had apparently overcome her terrible experiences enough to exert a loving influence among strangers. She loved Naaman and his family.

God's love is primarily concerned with the other's well-being, irrespective of the cost, and Naaman's little maid set about being a blessing. She was a light in a dark place, arresting the corruption around her, love as love had seldom been shown before. She wanted her master healed! If I had been in her position, I might have kept my precious information to myself! She showed such liberality of spirit in her ability to forgive the wrongs done to her that her words were heard by the king! Someone actually told him what she, a humble slave girl, had said! Here is a captured slave trying to help her captors, seeking to save their lives! That sort of attitude is bound to arrest the attention of a nonbelieving world. Instead of being glad her master had leprosy ("serves him right—I hope he dies slowly and painfully") she put her mouth to work and loudly testified to the power of her God to save him. Imagine, however, what would have happened if her life had not matched up to her message. Do you think her mistress or the king would have taken notice of her? Like Esther in the palace of Ahasuerus, Naaman's maid shone brightly—so brightly her message was taken seriously!

So what did she say that had such a profound impact on her hearers? She told them about the Israel of God and the God of Israel! "There is a prophet of the Lord in Israel," she confidently asserted, "who will heal my master of his leprosy!" This particular teenager spoke up with total confidence about Elisha and his God. She believed the people of God were just that—God's people—called of God to be a blessing to the whole world, including Naaman! She trusted Elisha to know what to do because he was in touch with the God who was real. How did she come by such virgin faith? Such heavenly audacity at such a young age? One can only surmise Naaman's little maid had responded to a believing home and to the influence of her parents who I'm sure had taken Deuteronomy 6:6-7 seriously.

> These commandments that I give you today are to be upon your hearts. Impress them on your children. Talk about them when you sit at home and when you walk along the road, when you lie down and when you get up.

This godly upbringing had resulted in her irrepressible beliefs in a God who was big enough for anything—even Naaman's leprosy.

In our day with the family disintegrating, we never know just how long we have to instill the truths of God into our children's lives, but we should not be complacent believing we have forever. In the end of the 20th century, Christian grandparents are very vital people. They also can play incredibly important roles in the education process. The god Rimmon reigned in Naaman's world. He was the god of "thunder." An angry, frightening deity that had no ability to forgive, to love, or to inspire. Naaman's little maid had a look at this religion and rejected it as thoroughly useless in her present predicament. Only the God of Israel could save, heal, change, and forgive. Her belief was bolstered by all she had heard of Jehovah's power demonstrated through Elisha's life and ministry already.

Hadn't Elisha been a great man with his Master too? Elijah was legendary and now his mantle had fallen on his chosen successor Elisha. Through him the waters of the Jordan had miraculously parted, a widow's tiny pot of oil had filled dozens of vessels, a boy had been raised from the dead, and 1,000 men had been fed with a few loaves of bread. No wonder Naaman's little maid found courage to witness to the power of her God! Over and over again God encouraged His people to think about, recall, and rehearse in the ears of future generations all His mighty works. Why? To remind them He was absolutely able to do all things for those who trusted Him. It was God's plan that Israel would soon turn the entire world toward His saving, healing, helping grace.

And so the king sent Naaman with a letter in his hand to Israel's king. Naaman took clothes, gold, and silver, and set off on his journey. When he arrived the king of Israel had a fit thinking this was a trick so that if the man was not healed, the king of Syria would have an excuse to declare war. On hearing what was happening, Elisha sent a message to the king telling him to send Naaman to him.

Coming to the prophet's house, Naaman was greeted by Elisha's servant who told him to dip seven times in the river Jordan and he would be healed. Naaman was furious. Why hadn't Elisha shown him the courtesy of greeting him himself. He believed the rivers of Syria were far superior to the muddy little Jordan anyway. Enraged he set off back home, but his servants persuaded him to listen to the prophet. It says much for the man that he swallowed his pride, listened to his servants, and did what Elisha told him to do! When he did, he was healed! He returned to Elisha at once to "pay" his doctor's bill, but Elisha talked with him refusing the gifts and money, wanting nothing to distract from the conversion of Naaman and God's part in it. Gehazi, Elisha's servant, however, followed Naaman secretly and with lies and a heart full of greed took the payment from him. Elisha, discerning what had happened, sadly told Gehazi that Naaman's leprosy would now cling to him. And so it did. In effect, Christian lepers abound! The leprosy of covetousness contaminates the soul, and one day will "break" out in unsightly sores for everyone to see if we are not daily cleansed by the Christ of Calvary.

Can you imagine the joy of Naaman's little maid when her master returned healed by Jehovah? Now she had an ally in that place. Now Naaman understood her heart, her bright eyes, and her loving, forgiving spirit. If we, like Naaman's little maid, will forgive as we have been forgiven, who knows if a Naaman will be the result! Then we will truly have changed our world!

•TALKING IT OVER•

Suggested Times

---

1. READ AND DISCUSS.   *15 minutes*
Read the passage of Scripture pertaining to the story (2 Kings 5). Discuss:
☐ The comparison of leprosy to sin
☐ Naaman's little maid
☐ Elisha's behavior
☐ Gehazi's actions

---

2. SHARE.   *15 minutes*
Can you share a part of this story that has been meaningful to you? How could we use this story to encourage others?

•PRAYING IT THROUGH•

Suggested Times

---

1. (On your own) Take time to praise God for saving circumstances He has engineered for you when trouble came. Praise God for the Elishas in your life who helped you to find cleansing for your sin.

8 minutes

---

2. (As a group) Pray for people who:
   □ Have a troubled past
   □ Need to forgive
   □ Need to be forgiven

7 minutes

---

3. (As a group) Pray for humble believers (like Naaman's little maid) who shine like a light in a dark place in:
   □ The Communist world
   □ The Muslim world

5 minutes

•DIGGING DEEPER•

Dorcas

Naaman's little maid and Dorcas knew the meaning and the beauty of service. They chose to make themselves a blessing to others. They were not discriminant in who were the recipients of their blessings. What lessons do they have for you?

1. Read Acts 9:36-43. Identify Joppa on a map and refer to the article on this New Testament city in a good Bible dictionary.

2. Look up the definition of *disciple* and list the major components. How often is it used of women in the New Testament?
   a lot

3. What was Dorcas reputed for and what were her spiritual gifts? What is the difference between Dorcas and your friend who volunteers for charitable and philanthropic causes? (cf. Eph. 2:10)
   good works
   she did it for God

4. From the text, who may have been the primary beneficiaries of Dorcas' ministry? (cf. James 1:27)
   poor people

5. Why did the disciples send for Peter in verse 38 and what was their expectation? (cf. vv. 32-34)
   To heal her

6. What does Peter's posture for prayer indicate about his attitude in prayer? What miracle do his words recall? (cf. Mark 5:41)
   He believed in the Power of God

7. What was the result of Dorcas being restored to life? How did this miracle affect the church?

It shows how strong God's power is

8. How does this story relate to the major themes in Acts?

Growth in the Church

9. In what ways did Dorcas exhibit Christlikeness?

That she died and was raised from the dead

10. The extension of her life, unawares to Dorcas, brought about revival (v. 42). Do you ever wish to extend your life and why?

?

11. The name *Dorcas* means "gazelle" and her life truly displayed the beauty and glory of the Lord. Does yours?

12. What did Dorcas and Naaman's little maid have in common? Do you share these characteristics? *They both showed God's love.*

For Further Study
1. Who helped establish the church in Joppa?
2. Do a word study of disciple.

•TOOL CHEST•
(A Suggested Optional Resource)

MY YEARS WITH CORRIE

Like both Naaman's little maid and Dorcas, Ellen de Kroon Stamps changed her world by being a servant. For nine years she was Corrie ten Boom's secretary and personal assistant, living with and accompanying Corrie throughout their travels across the globe. Her story is told in *My Years with Corrie* (Revell). Ellen changed her world with a listening ear, gentle counsel, quiet evangelism, and an obedient heart. She was often a "light in a dark place." Many times in Ellen's life, both Corrie and the Lord asked her to attempt the unattemptable — things beyond what she believed she could do. Each time she rose to the occasion and God blessed her with fruit. Her transparent testimony will draw you to the Father when you page through the personal lessons God taught her about trust, death, singleness, and much more.